Lizards look for food at night.

The owl watches from his tree.

Coyotes howl at the moon.

The owl watches from his tree.

Roadrunners race after a mouse.

The owl watches from his tree.

Snakes slither across the ground.

The owl watches from his tree.

Tortoises crawl over the sand.

The owl watches from his tree.

Then it's quiet in the desert

and the owl watches from his tree.